USING THIS BOOK

*One of the best ways of helping children learn to read is to read stories to them and with them. This way they learn what **reading** is, and they will gradually come to recognize many words and begin to read for themselves.*

First, read the story on the left-hand pages aloud to the child.

Reread the story as often as the child enjoys hearing it. Talk about the pictures as you go.

Later the child will be able to read the words under the pictures on the right-hand pages.

The pages at the back of the book will give you some ideas for helping your child to read.

© Text and layout SHEILA McCULLAGH MCMLXXXV
© In publication LADYBIRD BOOKS LTD MCMLXXXV
Loughborough, England
LADYBIRD BOOKS, INC.
Lewiston, Maine 04240 U.S.A.

Printed in England

Mrs. Pitter-Patter and the Magician

written by SHEILA McCULLAGH
illustrated by MARK CHADWICK

This book belongs to:

_____

Ladybird Books

Mrs. Pitter-Patter lived
at one end of Puddle Lane.
Mrs. Pitter-Patter
was always telling everyone else
what they ought to do.
One day, Mrs. Pitter-Patter
went out.
The sun was shining
and the sky was blue.
Mrs. Pitter-Patter went
up the lane.

Mrs. Pitter-Patter
went up the lane.

She saw Miss Baker making bread,
and told her that
she ought to make a cake.
Mrs. Pitter-Patter went on
up the lane,
and Miss Baker put the bread
in the oven.

She saw Miss Baker.

She saw Mr. Puffle.
Mr. Puffle was painting his door green,
and she told him that
he ought to paint it white.
Mrs. Pitter-Patter went on
up the lane,
and Mr. Puffle opened another can
of green paint.

She saw Mr. Puffle.

She saw Pedro and Rosa.
Pedro and Rosa lived
in Puddle Lane.
They were playing with a ball.
Mrs. Pitter-Patter told them
that they ought to get
a jump rope instead.
"And you mustn't play in the lane,"
Mrs. Pitter-Patter said.
"You should play in the garden
of the old house."
Mrs. Pitter-Patter went on
up the lane,
and Pedro threw the ball to Rosa.

She saw
Pedro and Rosa.

She saw Davy and Sarah.
Davy and Sarah were jumping rope,
and Mrs. Pitter-Patter told them
that they ought to play ball.
"And you shouldn't play
in the lane," she said.
"You should play in the garden
of the old house."
Mrs. Pitter-Patter went on
up the lane,
and Davy and Sarah
went on jumping.

She saw
Davy and Sarah.

She saw Mr. Gotobed
sitting in the sunshine,
and she told him that
he ought to be in bed.
Mrs. Pitter-Patter went on
up the lane.
Mr. Gotobed shut his eyes and dozed,
as he sat in his chair
in the sunshine.

She saw Mr. Gotobed.

Mrs. Pitter-Patter came
to the end of Puddle Lane.
There was a very old house
at the end of the lane,
with gates leading into the garden.
Mrs. Pitter-Patter stopped
at the gates.
She looked into the garden.

Mrs. Pitter-Patter
looked into the garden.

She saw an old man sitting
under a tree. He was fast asleep
in a chair.

Mrs. Pitter-Patter didn't know it,
but the old man was a magician.

Mrs. Pitter-Patter opened the gate,
and went into the garden.

Mrs. Pitter-Patter
saw the Magician
in the garden.

Mrs. Pitter-Patter went up
to the Magician.
"You shouldn't be fast asleep
at this time of day," she said.
"Wake up and do something!"

Mrs. Pitter-Patter
went up
to the Magician.

The Magician woke up.
He looked at Mrs. Pitter-Patter.
"What do you want me to do?"
he asked.
"Anything useful,"
said Mrs. Pitter-Patter.
"Very well, I will,"
said the Magician.
"I'll do something **very** useful."
And he snapped his fingers.

The Magician woke up.

The very next moment,
Mrs. Pitter-Patter found herself
getting smaller.
"Oh dear, oh dear!"
cried Mrs. Pitter-Patter.
"You're turning into a giant!"

Mrs. Pitter-Patter
and the Magician

"**I'm** not growing bigger,
but **you're** growing smaller,"
said the Magician.
Mrs. Pitter-Patter was
so small by this time,
that the Magician had to pick her up
and hold her in his hand,
so that he could talk to her.

Mrs. Pitter-Patter
and the Magician

"Put me down! Put me down!"
cried Mrs. Pitter-Patter.
"If I put you down, will you go
away and not bother me?"
asked the Magician.
"I'll go away. I'll never come back!"
said Mrs. Pitter-Patter.

"Put me down!
Put me down!"
cried Mrs. Pitter-Patter.

So the Magician put
Mrs. Pitter-Patter down
on the grass,
and she ran through the grass
to the gate.

Mrs. Pitter-Patter
ran to the gate.

She went under the gate,
and out into Puddle Lane.

Mrs. Pitter-Patter
went under the gate.

But as soon as she was safely
back in Puddle Lane,
Mrs. Pitter-Patter was herself again.
She was just as tall
as she wanted to be.

Mrs. Pitter-Patter
was herself again.

Mrs. Pitter-Patter
ran down the lane.
She wanted to get home
as fast as she could.
She met Pedro and Rosa,
and Davy and Sarah.
They were all playing in the lane.
"Play in the lane if you like,"
said Mrs. Pitter-Patter,
"but never, **never**, NEVER
go into the garden of the old house!"
And she ran home to make herself
a cup of tea.

Mrs. Pitter-Patter
ran home.

Notes for the parent/teacher

When you have read the story, go back to the beginning. Look at each picture and talk about it. Point to the caption below, and read it aloud yourself. Run your finger under the words as you read, so that the child learns that reading goes from left to right. (You don't have to say this in so many words.

Children learn many useful things about reading just by reading with you, and it is often better to let them learn by experience rather than by explanation.)

The next time you go through the book, encourage the child to read the words and sentences under the illustrations. Don't

Mrs Pitter-Patter dropped the tail with a yell. She made such a noise, that she woke Mr Gotobed, who was fast asleep in bed in the house at the end of the lane.

Mr. Gotobed woke up.

rush in with a word before he* has time to think, but don't leave him struggling for too long. Always encourage him to feel that he is reading successfully, praising him when he does well, and avoiding criticism.

Now turn back to the beginning, and print the child's name in the space on the title page, using ordinary, not capital letters. Let him watch you print it: this is another useful experience.

*Children enjoy hearing the same story many times. Read this one as often as the child likes hearing it. The more opportunities he has to look at the illustrations and **read** the captions with you, the more he will come to recognize the words. Don't worry if he **remembers** rather than **reads** the captions. This is a normal stage in learning.*

If you have a number of books, let the child choose which story he would like to hear again.

---

* In order to avoid the continual "he or she," "him or her," the child is referred to in this book as "he." However, the stories are equally appropriate for boys and girls.

Ask: *Who is this?*

Mr.
Puffle

Mrs.
Pitter-Patter

Ask: *Who is this?*

the
Magician

Mr.
Gotobed

41

Rosa

Pedro

Davy

Sarah

There are several books in this Stage about the same characters. All the books in each Stage are separate stories and are written at the same reading level.

The lists below show other titles available in Stages 1 and 2.

Stage 1

2 Tessa and the Magician

3 The Magic Box

4 Mrs. Pitter-Patter and the Magician

5 The Vanishing Monster

Have you read these stories about other characters in Puddle Lane?

Stage 1

6 *The Wideawake Mice* is the story of a family of toy mice who find that everything changes after the Magician visits the toy store.

9 *The Tale of a Tail* is another story about Mrs. Pitter-Patter, and what happens when she pulls a monster's tail.